Rochester History

SPRING 2026

Rochester History

A publication of the Rochester Public Library
in partnership with Rochester Institute of Technology

Volume 83, Issue 2

STAFF
Editors: Christine L. Ridarsky and Rebecca Edwards
Assistant Editor: Emily Morry

Contents

DIRECTOR'S CORNER

Urban renewal marked a pivotal chapter in the evolution of American cities, and, as Benjamin Comeau and Katie Eggers Comeau demonstrate in "Saved by Play: The Rise and Fall of Urban Renewal in Rochester's Southeast Loop," Rochester was no exception. In Rochester, these initiatives reshaped not only the physical landscape but also the dynamics of community life. Entire neighborhoods were altered or erased, longstanding social networks were disrupted, and public institutions were forced to redefine their roles in response to these sweeping changes.

The history of the Rochester Public Library itself is an institution whose history is deeply interwoven with these cycles of disruption, reinvention, and community resilience. Few places illustrate the promises, losses, and ongoing consequences of urban renewal quite as vividly as our libraries. The Central Library of Rochester & Monroe County, situated in the heart of the city just down the road from the Southeast Loop neighborhood that the Comeaus discuss, has been both a witness to and a participant in these transformations. The construction of the Rundel Memorial Building in 1936, and later the 1997 opening of the Bausch & Lomb Public Library Building, reflect the evolving civic priorities of their eras, from monumental New Deal optimism to late-century commitments to modernization and urban reinvestment. Now the Central Library is undergoing significant restoration and stands mere blocks away from projects aimed at restoring community on sites where urban renewal once disrupted neighborhoods, displaced families, and paved over culture to make way for modern commercial corridors.

Libraries, by design, are spaces of complexity, serving as both repositories of memory and catalysts for civic imagination. Through our Local History & Genealogy Division, we work to preserve Rochester's urban renewal story and make it accessible to anyone seeking to understand how past decisions continue to shape the present. Increasingly, patrons use our resources to inform efforts around neighborhood revitalization, community planning, and justice-centered development.

As Rochester moves into a new era—one marked by renewed investment, advances in technology, and vibrant public discourse—the lessons of the past are more vital than ever. Understanding the history of urban renewal not only grounds us in the lived experiences of our communities, but it also equips us to make more informed, collaborative decisions about the city we are building, and sometimes rebuilding, together.

I am grateful to Benjamin Comeau and Katie Eggers Comeau for their painstaking research and to *Rochester History* for dedicating space to the topic of urban renewal and providing a platform where we can all deepen our shared understanding of this aspect of Rochester's past. The library remains committed to supporting this work by preserving the record, facilitating access, and welcoming all who seek to explore how the city we know today came to be. ■

Emily Clasper
Director, Rochester Public Library and the Monroe County Library System

LETTER FROM THE EDITORS

Dear reader,

Welcome to our spring issue! With appreciation to our book reviewer, Matt Dallos, this issue offers, in his words, a tour of Rochester's "environmental, economic, and social particularities." Dallos used the phrase to praise Camden Burd's 2024 book, *The Roots of Flower City: Horticulture, Empire, and the Remaking of Rochester, New York.*

Any consideration of Rochester's environmental and economic particularities must include the Erie Canal, and this issue is no different. Historian Rich Newman interviewed Mark Ferrara about his book, *The Raging Erie: Life and Labor Along the Erie Canal.* A lightly edited transcript of their conversation appears in this issue. For a more in-depth version, their conversation is available to our subscribers to stream on the digital edition.

Harold J. Schuler introduces us to the social particularity of Rochester's nineteenth-century past in the latest installment of the ROC Artifact. He offers us a humble business card, a small item powerfully evocative of a time and a place. This rare card is truly remarkable. It is a card for a Black-owned business in Rochester in 1860, a grocery store briefly owned and operated by Frederick Douglass's sons, Lewis and Frederick Jr. Why they ran the business and why they stopped is Schuler's story to share.

Finally, this is not the only story that features a familial twist. In a first for us, our main article was authored by a mother-and-son team. Benjamin Comeau and Katie Eggers Comeau bring us "Saved by Play: The Rise and Fall of Urban Renewal in Rochester's Southeast Loop." They explore urban renewal and its lasting legacies of racial inequity in the city of Rochester, but theirs is a story with a twist of its own. The planned housing project that they painstakingly follow failed to materialize in the southeast corner of the city; the area nonetheless experienced a sort of urban renewal, though of a completely unplanned kind. The Strong National Museum of Play was built in the neighborhood instead. In this issue, economic particularities and historical contingencies abound.

Enjoy! ■

Christine L. Ridarsky and Rebecca Edwards
Editors

Saved by Play: The Rise and Fall of Urban Renewal in Rochester's Southeast Loop

Benjamin Comeau and Katie Eggers Comeau

In June 2023, the Strong National Museum of Play opened a 90,000-square-foot expansion that increased the size of the institution to 375,000 square feet. The museum's vibrantly colored, visually arresting addition was the most notable in a series of projects that refashioned its downtown Rochester, New York, neighborhood into the "Neighborhood of Play." Anchored by the enlarged museum, the development included new apartments and townhouses, restaurants, a rainbow-colored parking garage, and a hotel. The Strong has long been heralded as one of the greatest children's museums in the country, housing interactive exhibits and experiences, as well as the National Toy Hall of Fame—all designed to engage people of every age—but the addition added to its appeal. In 2024, the museum welcomed almost 700,000 guests, and it hopes to increase annual visitation to one million by 2026.

None of this was envisioned by the mid-twentieth-century proponents of urban renewal who set out to improve what was then viewed as a run-down area of the city. They had no intention of attracting a world-class museum to the southeast quadrant of downtown. Their plan for the area they referred to as the "Southeast Loop" called for replacing a century-old residential neighborhood, which they thought was beyond saving, with a modern, dense enclave of

Benjamin Comeau is a student at the University of Pennsylvania, where he is studying philosophy, politics, and economics with a minor in urban real estate and development. He expects to graduate in May 2026. He is excited to start his career in real estate development after graduation, hoping to specialize in urban infill projects.

Katie Eggers Comeau is the senior architectural historian at Bero Architecture, located just inside the former Inner Loop. She has a BA in humanities from Yale University and an MS in historic preservation from the University of Pennsylvania. As a native of the Rochester area, she visited the Strong Museum soon after it opened and vividly remembers long cases full of dollhouses, dolls, and toy soldiers; she also remembers bringing her son to the museum for the first time as a special treat on his first birthday.

high-rise apartment buildings and townhouses intended to attract middle-class residents who would anchor a revival of the city's core. These plans failed due to a series of misjudgments. The museum, opened in 1982, was a lucky rescue to a botched project.

The immediate post–World War II period, as the national and local economy recovered from the Great Depression and the war, was a time of optimism for some segments of Rochester society. Reflecting on the postwar period from the vantage point of the early 1960s, Rochester City Historian Blake McKelvey noted, "As industry seized its postwar and then its cold war opportunities with renewed vigor, the city experienced a resurgence of confidence."[1] Local leaders envisioned sustained population and economic growth, which would support ambitious plans to remake the city's transportation system and its housing stock. Prosperity and opportunity had never been equally available to all residents of Rochester, and the city's postwar projects both shined a light on and exacerbated the inequities. Repeatedly, it was the city's most-disadvantaged residents whose lives were uprooted by highway and housing projects, even as planners claimed to want to improve those citizens' living conditions. These dynamics played out in dramatic fashion in the Southeast Loop project, which was unveiled in 1966 and came to an ignominious end more than a decade later.

Remaking Postwar Rochester: The Inner Loop and Midtown Plaza, 1946-1965

The first transformative plan for postwar Rochester focused on making the city's transportation system more convenient for the private automobile. By 1946, planners from the City of Rochester and from New York State, eager to take advantage of newly available state funding for highway construction, were separately formulating plans for arterial highways in Rochester; both plans were unveiled in September 1947.[2] City and state officials came to a compromise on the route in late 1948.[3] The plan they devised took the form of a ring-and-spoke system. At the center, ringing the city's central business district around Main Street and the Genesee River, the plan envisioned a highway in the shape of an irregular oval, known from the start as the Inner Loop. Transportation planners considered the center of the city to be the most problematic area in the region, in which automobile travel was already unacceptably slow and likely to become worse given expected population and business growth. The Inner Loop was conceived as a partially sunken, partially elevated, limited-access highway that would keep through traffic off city streets and provide a quick way in and out of downtown. Arterial "spokes" were to connect the Inner Loop

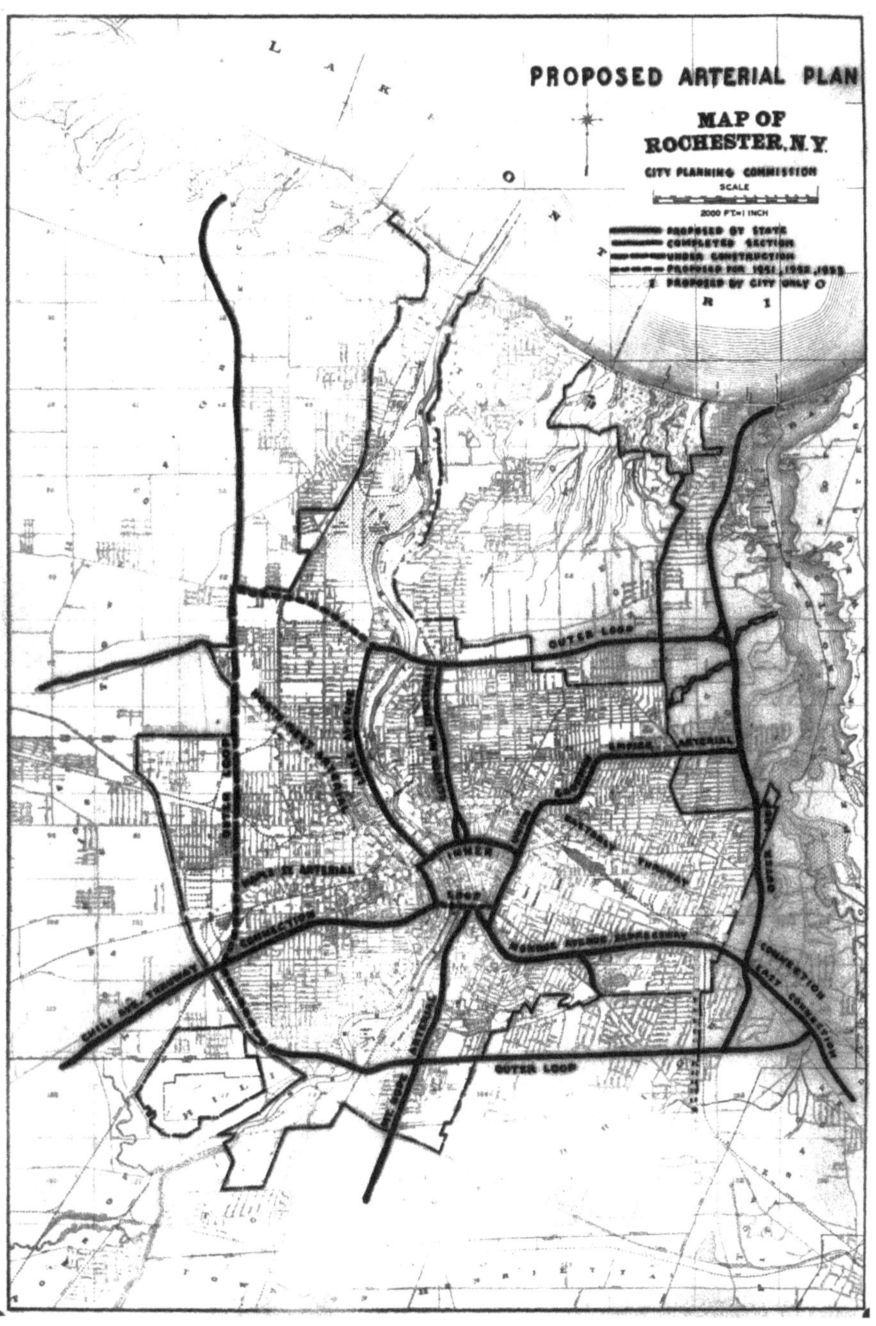

The proposal to reshape Rochester's transportation network by building a web of arterial and ring highways, including the Inner Loop, had lasting consequences on both the city and the suburbs. *City of Rochester.*

to an Outer Loop, a much larger ring around the city's outskirts—largely to be accomplished by increasing the capacity of existing roads. The compromise plan became official in February 1949.[4]

Construction of the Inner Loop comprised five sections, the first begun in 1952 and the last completed in 1965. The first two sections were on the west side of the Genesee River. In 1956, work began on the third section, a sunken highway extending a half mile from the Genesee River eastward to the intersection of Union and George streets. This portion of the Inner Loop, completed in 1958, later formed the southern boundary of the Southeast Loop project. Demolition work began on the fourth section, the northernmost piece of the loop, in 1957; this complicated stretch of highway was not completed until 1962. In the same year, demolition crews moved to the final section, from Union and George Streets to Scio Street. The south half of this section, completed in 1965, later defined the eastern edge of the Southeast Loop area.[5]

A second transformative project was Midtown Plaza, one of the nation's first downtown indoor shopping malls. That project, situated a few blocks north of the eventual Southeast Loop area, was developed in the late 1950s to effect revitalization of the traditional Main Street commercial corridor. The modest initial concept, as presented by the owners of major downtown department stores, was to build a parking garage coordinated with the Inner Loop, in an effort to keep a suburbanizing populace shopping downtown by creating a car-friendly environment that was also pleasant and safe for pedestrians. As designed by architect Victor Gruen, the project became much more ambitious, featuring an enclosed plaza connecting existing department stores, a new office tower, and new retail space, all atop an underground parking garage. Midtown Plaza opened to great fanfare in 1962.[6]

Housing for the Postwar City

The goals of modernizing the city's transportation system and strengthening its commercial core overlapped with other planning priorities, particularly the improvement of housing conditions. Local activists and reformers had been advocating throughout the twentieth century for public and private action to relieve housing shortages and improve housing conditions in the city's most overcrowded neighborhoods, to little effect. During the Great Depression and World War II, proponents who favored aggressive efforts to create new housing urged city leaders to follow the example of other urban areas by creating a housing authority with broad powers to construct publicly funded housing.

Champions of this approach included African American journalist and historian Howard W. Coles, nurse and social investigator Elsie Scott Kilpatrick, Helen Jones of the League of Women Voters, and workers at various settlement houses. These advocates thought government intervention was the best way to create better housing, particularly for Black and immigrant populations, many of whom lived in the city's worst housing.[7] In Rochester, however, the business, banking, and real estate communities consistently opposed government intervention—which they characterized as a threat to the private housing market—and managed for years to stymie efforts to take advantage of federal funding for housing redevelopment.[8]

The private interests that blocked government intervention in the housing market were acting to protect a system that had created and maintained severe inequities in housing in Rochester and its suburbs. Federal, state, and local policies and practices incentivized the construction of houses for white Americans in neighborhoods that explicitly or implicitly barred African Americans and, sometimes, other minority groups. Realtors were forbidden by their code of ethics from showing houses in predominantly white neighborhoods to potential buyers who were not white; banking policies discouraged lending to African Americans or investing in neighborhoods with high concentrations of African American and/or immigrant residents; restrictive covenants written into deeds forbade owners from selling to members of minority groups; homeowners hostile to integration engaged in vandalism and other tactics, letting potential Black neighbors know they were not welcome, regardless of their professional status or income level. The suburban towns ringing Rochester adopted zoning practices such as minimum house and lot sizes to ensure that only single-family houses for middle- and upper-middle-income families could be built.[9] These policies and practices resulted in a highly segregated metropolitan area, with newer housing, both in the city and in inner-ring suburbs, restricted to white residents, while a growing population of African American residents found limited and overpriced options concentrated in two parts of the city: the Third Ward (Corn Hill) and the Fifth and Seventh Wards (sometimes called the "Near Northeast"). Puerto Rican residents, who began moving to Rochester in sizable numbers in the early 1950s, also found limited options. These neighborhoods had some of the oldest housing in the city, and because banks would not underwrite mortgages or home-improvement loans in these supposedly risky areas, residents were at the mercy of landlords who charged exorbitant rents for overcrowded housing that was often in shockingly poor condition.[10]

In 1949, more than a decade after many cities (including nearby Buffalo) began building public housing, Rochester undertook its first publicly funded housing project. The initial plan to build on a vacant site on the north edge of the city near Franklin High School was stymied by opposition from the white ethnics living in the surrounding neighborhood. Eventually, the housing complex known as the Hanover Houses was built in the Baden-Ormond area of the Seventh Ward, where six acres were cleared and a series of seven-story apartment towers, opened in 1953, were built. The complex, which initially contained 140 apartments (later subdivided to create 392 units), displaced 175 families, only 40 of whom were qualified and interested in living in the new towers; most of the rest were ineligible because their incomes were too high. African American families displaced by the project struggled to find housing elsewhere.[11] While the Hanover Houses initially were praised by some housing advocates for offering a large-scale solution to a massive problem, the complex quickly came under fire for creating dangerous, overcrowded, and generally undesirable living conditions. By the time the Hanover Houses were demolished in the early 1980s, they were universally considered a failure.

Some housing advocates initially saw the Hanover Houses as a potential model for large-scale, government-led solutions to the housing problem; others saw a cautionary tale and pushed for a more incremental approach focused on repair and rehabilitation of existing housing. In 1955, the Rochester City Council tried to have it both ways, placating those who favored more aggressive action by creating a housing authority but appeasing those who wanted a more conservative approach by calling it the "Rochester Housing Authority and Rehabilitation Commission."[12] Nominally two entities made up of the same five members, they diverged to pursue separate approaches. The Rehabilitation Commission had under its purview the pursuit of a rehabilitation, or "neighborhood conservation," approach. It was also specifically tasked with overseeing improvement of the 60-acre Baden-Ormond area surrounding the recently built Hanover Houses.[13]

The Rehabilitation Commission's efforts to focus on rehabilitation and neighborhood improvement initially seemed promising. In April 1956, inspectors from the Rehabilitation Commission began a series of house-by-house inspections, starting in the Third Ward, where they reported that about 60 percent of the housing units were "unsafe or unsanitary."[14] As the inspectors made their way from ward to ward, their goal was to encourage owners to voluntarily make the necessary repairs to correct code violations, and they initially reported excellent

The Hanover Houses, located off of Joseph Avenue between Vienna Street and Herman Street (now Upper Falls Blvd), were Rochester's first large-scale housing complex built to provide housing to families with low incomes; constructed in the 1950s, they were demolished in the 1980s. *City of Rochester.*

success. While they found violations in well over half of the dwelling units they inspected, most owners brought those units into compliance voluntarily.[15] The Rehabilitation Commission tried to work in partnership with residents and actively encouraged citizen efforts to improve their neighborhoods by promoting the creation of community-led Neighborhood Improvement Councils. These groups met regularly with Rehabilitation Commission representatives and coordinated their efforts to identify and address problematic properties and landlords.[16] As the Rehabilitation Commission continued its regular inspections, it increasingly relied not just on the goodwill of property owners but also on legal mechanisms for requiring compliance. The Rehabilitation Commission could refer property owners to the district attorney's office and corporation counsel (the city's legal office) regarding statutory (or code) violations. It also had the authority to call hearings at which they would hear testimony from both aggrieved tenants and recalcitrant landlords. A handful of owners were brought before public hearings, and an even smaller number were compelled to make repairs.[17]

The Rehabilitation Commission and the Manhattan-Savannah Neighborhood

One of the areas the Rehabilitation Commission targeted was a portion of the city's Fourth Ward inside the partially built Inner Loop. This was an area of modestly sized, mostly wood-framed housing, much of which was nearly 100 years old when the Rehabilitation Commission's inspectors visited. The commission's outreach efforts seemed to pay off at first. The Manhattan-Savannah Neighborhood Council (also known as the Manhattan-Savannah Area Improvement Council), named for two prominent streets in the neighborhood, was formed in 1956 and focused on problems stemming from the proliferation of absentee landlords.[18] In 1957, residents formed another new organization, the Manhattan-Savannah Garden Club, which held two garden contests in its inaugural year. As the chair of the garden club, Mrs. Dorothy A. Brown, of 32 Savannah Street, noted, "We're just hoping we can make a real improvement in our surroundings, and if we all keep up the good work that has been started, we will."[19] The neighborhood had its own newsletter, *The Fourth Ward Neighbor*, later *The Fourth Ward Neighbor and the Southsider*, which shared information about clean-up days, neighborhood association meetings, and other items of interest to the residents who maintained hope that they could still make a positive difference in their neighborhood's condition and future.[20]

In 1958, the Manhattan-Savannah Improvement Council made news when

This circa 1967 map details the area in question bounded by the Inner Loop on the east and south, Clinton Avenue South on the west, and Court Street, James Street, and East Avenue on the north. *Rochester Public Library Local History & Genealogy Division.*

members of the group appeared at a Rehabilitation Commission hearing to testify about how deteriorating properties were affecting not just the tenants of those properties, but the neighborhood as a whole.[21] Their concerted efforts not to let their neighborhood, or their neighbors, fall victim to the neglect of absentee landlords seemed to be a model for other neighborhoods facing similar issues and seemed to be having a positive impact. The concerned members of the Manhattan-Savannah Improvement Council and the Manhattan-Savannah Garden Club may have thought they could persuade absentee landlords to become more considerate and encourage their neighbors to plant gardens and, in doing so, ensure a brighter future for their neighborhood. They may have believed that their allies in City Hall would enforce laws meant to crack down on code violations and force owners to clean up deteriorated properties. They may not have realized that their houses were already in the sights of planners who were starting to develop a completely different vision for the future of one of Rochester's oldest neighborhoods.

The Manhattan Tract Before Urban Renewal

In 1964, city planners began using the term "Southeast Loop" to refer to the area residents had only recently begun calling the "Manhattan-Savannah neighborhood"; the new term must have been jarring to residents. Before the 1950s, the neighborhood didn't even have a name, which was not unusual: Before the 1970s, sections of the city were most commonly known by their political ward numbers (a few of which, notably the Third and Nineteenth, have remained recognizable decades after the ward system was officially abolished).[22] While the origins of the street names in the neighborhood are unknown, one of the names, Manhattan Street, can be traced back to the tracts laid out and subdivided by real estate speculators in the first half of the nineteenth century—the Manhattan Square Tract, roughly from Chestnut to William Streets, and the Manhattan Tract, roughly from William to Union Streets. Historical maps show that the major streets in the two tracts were at least planned by the late 1820s; by midcentury, they had been subdivided into residential-sized lots and were sparsely settled. Residential construction in the area accelerated as the city's

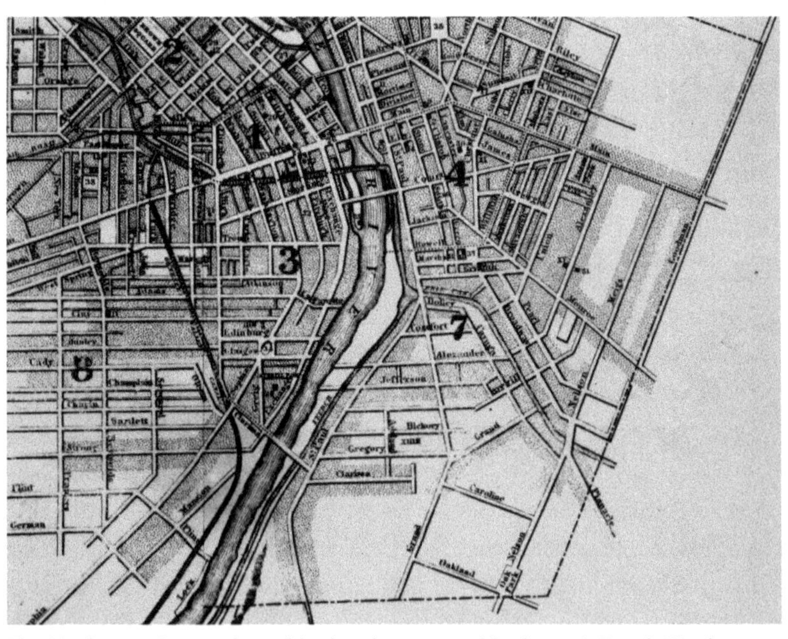

The Manhattan-Savannah neighborhood was part of Rochester's Fourth Ward, located just to the east (right) of the number 4 in this 1849 map of Rochester. Silas Cornell, *Map of the City of Rochester* (Jerome & Bro., 1849). *Rochester Public Library Local History & Genealogy Division Map Collection.*

population grew in the second half of the nineteenth century. By 1900, most lots were filled with wood-frame houses, and Monroe Avenue, at the south end of the two tracts, was lined with masonry mixed-use and apartment buildings.

The 1950 US Census provides a midcentury snapshot of the area. To take one block as an example, Enumeration District 69-27, Block 6, was located exactly where the Strong sits today, bounded by Broadway (formerly William Street), George Street, Manhattan Street, and Monroe Avenue. In total, 424 people lived in this one-block area, in 174 dwelling units, which included both detached houses and apartment buildings. Only 5 dwelling units were vacant; of the remaining 169, about 89 percent of heads of household were born in the United States. The remainder represented a broad mix: Four were from Canada, four from China, three from Greece, and one each from Finland, Scotland, England, Germany, Ireland, Italy, and Holland. Other than the members of the four families from China, all other residents of the block were recorded in the census as white. The people living on this one block comprised a variety of family types: nuclear families consisting of parents and children; single people

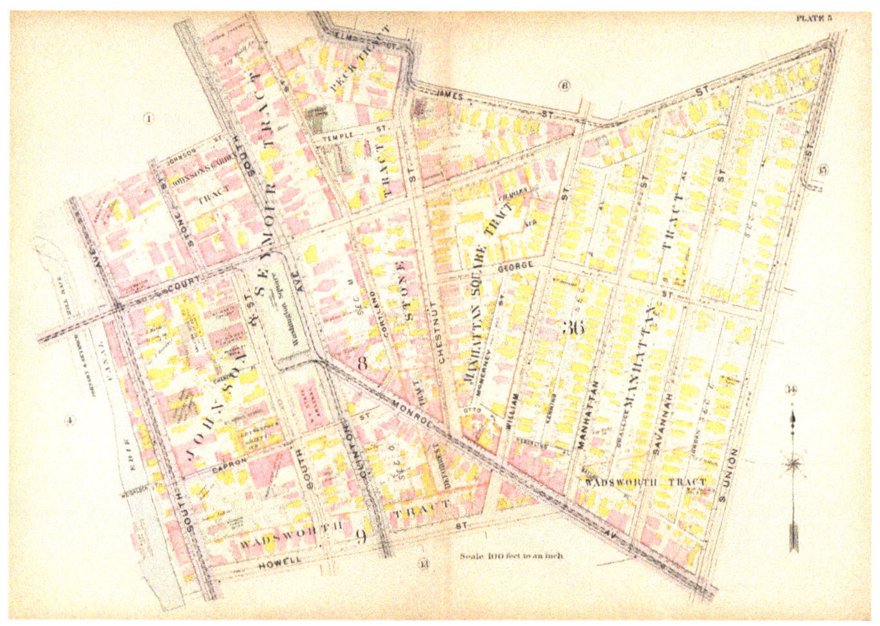

By the turn of the twentieth century, the Manhattan-Savannah neighborhood (shown on this plat map as the "Manhattan Tract," was almost fully built out, its residential streets lined with wood-framed houses. *Plat Map of the City of Rochester* (J. M. Lathrop & Co., 1900). *Rochester Public Library Local History & Genealogy Division Map Collection.*

of all ages; couples without children; unmarried partners; divorced or widowed adults, sometimes living with a child, partner, or sibling; and a few multigenerational families.

While maps show that most buildings on Broadway, Manhattan Street, and George Street were built as one- or two-story detached houses or side-by-side doubles, it was rare that these were still being used as single-family units by 1950. More than 80 percent of the single-family houses and duplexes were divided into multiple units. Many households included lodgers as a source of extra income. Residents of this block were employed in a variety of blue-collar jobs. They worked in bars, restaurants, factories, the building trades, theaters, department stores, and hotels. There were a few teachers, nurses, small-business owners, and even a zookeeper. They ranged in age from infants to octogenarians, and the average head of household was fifty. Families in which two or more members were employed were common, as were households headed by females.[23] The residents of this block, along with all of the neighbors in this enclave, were already seeing their neighborhood changing. Over the next two decades, it would transform even more dramatically, until eventually the homes and even the streets on which they lived were erased from the map altogether. Few of those who had lived there in 1950 remained to see it, however: Of the 174 houses and apartments on the block, only 12 had the same occupants in 1960 as in 1950, and only 4 of those had the same occupants in 1971, by which time the streets and houses around them had begun to disappear.[24]

When streets in the Manhattan-Savannah area received media attention in the 1950s, it was increasingly in the context of disturbing trends and changing demographics. A newspaper article in 1955 noted that this was one of two neighborhoods where "chronic police-case alcoholics" were clustered, living in "cheap hotels" and "cheap flops." The other area cited for its high rate of chronic alcoholism was Front Street, a section of the city near the Genesee River that was soon to be cleared in another urban renewal project, adding its residents to the increasing number of Rochesterians who were displaced.[25]

Articles in 1955 and 1961 decried housing discrimination and the exorbitant rents that landlords were charging the Manhattan-Savannah neighborhood's growing Puerto Rican and African American populations. In the early 1950s, the area between Court Street, Monroe Avenue, and Union Street South—the exact area later known as the Southeast Loop—was one of the two areas of the city with the largest proportion of Puerto Rican residents.[26] Rochester's Puerto

Rican–born population was just beginning to burgeon, having grown from about 200 in 1952 to almost 4,000 in 1955.[27] Landlords in many neighborhoods refused to rent to Puerto Rican tenants, and while some in the area around Savannah and Manhattan Streets would, they charged high rents for poorly maintained, overcrowded houses: "It's not unusual for a family to pay $17 a week for a single room. Toilet facilities are often shared by several families and hot running water is a rarity. On George and Manhattan streets you find as many as six or seven families occupying as many small two-room apartments in a house. Rickety staircases, peeling plaster, shattered window panes—all the signs of neglect and decay are present."[28] At the time, $17 per week for a single room with a shared bath and no hot water would have been considered exorbitant. Residents of other city neighborhoods paid a similar price for three- or four-room apartments with a kitchen, private bathroom, and garage—often with utilities included.[29]

African Americans also began moving into the Fourth Ward in substantial numbers in the 1950s. Most were either new to the Rochester area, having just moved from the South during the Great Migration, or had been displaced from the Baden-Ormond area for construction of the Hanover Houses or the subsequent clearance project. These new residents encountered the same challenges as their Puerto Rican neighbors as landlords took advantage of their similarly desperate search for housing and overcharged them for poorly maintained apartments. The east side of Manhattan Street from Court Street to George Street, whose seventeen houses were occupied solely by white residents in 1950, was home to six African American families by 1961. A survey found that these families generally paid twice as much in rent as their white neighbors did, despite living in similar houses in similar or worse condition.[30]

With Inner Loop construction underway and an influx of new residents exacerbating already overcrowded conditions, it is little wonder that the Manhattan-Savannah area underwent rapid turnover in the 1950s and early 1960s. Absentee landlords had little impetus to maintain properties that were in the path of, or adjacent to, highway construction, and they had every incentive to squeeze every dollar of rent they could from desperate tenants with few options. These were the conditions that the Rehabilitation Commission, and the related Manhattan-Savannah Neighborhood Improvement Council, were trying to reverse in the late 1950s. By 1960, however, planners were starting to think differently about how to improve the neighborhood.

Manhattan-Savannah Becomes the Southeast Loop

Before construction of the Inner Loop, Rochester's principal commercial core was a nebulously defined area along and near Main Street, both east and west of the Genesee River. The Inner Loop changed Rochesterians' perceptions of, and language about, their city by clearly defining the area inside the loop as "downtown," or the "central business district," as distinct from the formerly contiguous residential neighborhoods just outside the new highway.

The "Manhattan-Savannah" neighborhood, once understood to be part of the "Fourth Ward," was now part of "downtown." Once "downtown" had a definite shape and clear boundary, it became the subject of intense planning activity, funded by new federal grant programs that encouraged municipalities to undertake long-term, comprehensive planning to underpin their urban renewal activities. Rochester tapped into these federal funding sources to embark upon a series of studies and plans in the 1960s that laid out new ideas for the city's

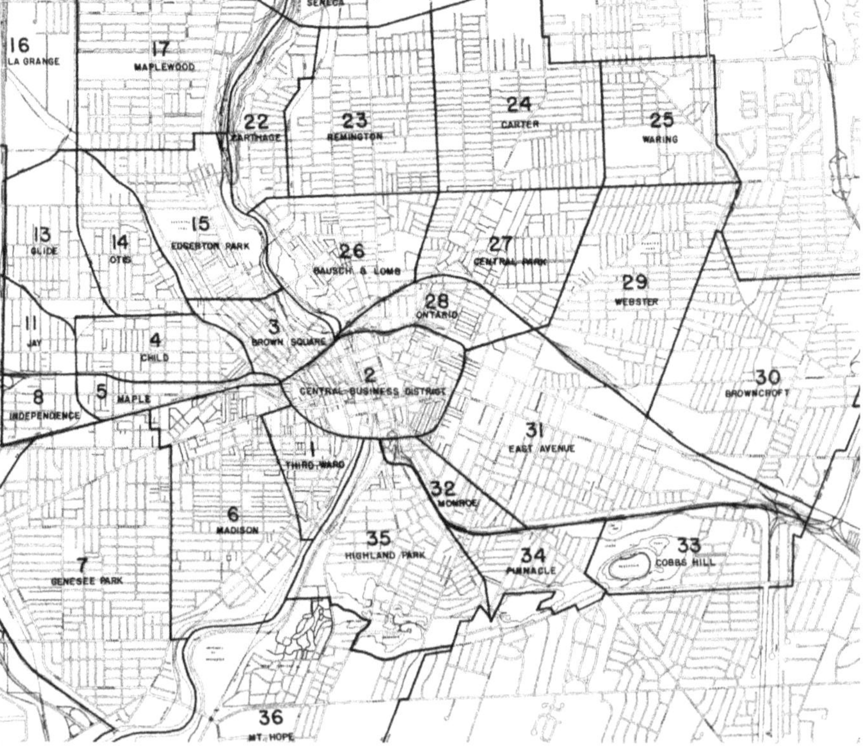

The construction of the Inner Loop created a clearly defined downtown area, labeled on this map from the 1963 *Community Renewal Program* as the "Central Business District." *Community Renewal Program, Rochester, New York, 1963 (City of Rochester, 1965).*

future. As a 1965 editorial noted about this period, "Sorting out the paper blizzard of plans to re-do downtown Rochester is about as easy as eating Jell-O with chopsticks."[31]

In 1960, the City Planning Commission hired a consultant to analyze the real estate market in the "Inner Loop Area." The consultant provided recommendations concerning various types of potential development including commercial, industrial, and residential. The study found that housing available within the Inner Loop compared unfavorably with that of the city as a whole, in that the percentage of units that were rented rather than owner-occupied was much higher (89 percent in the Inner Loop, compared to 48 percent in the city as a whole) and that one-third of the dwellings in the Inner Loop lacked a private bathroom or were otherwise in "dilapidated" condition (versus 9 percent of the city as a whole). Rejecting the incremental approach to individual property improvement, the consultant proposed a new strategy for downtown housing:

> Since virtually all of the housing within the inner loop is relatively old, with a high ratio of rental occupancy and a significant portion in a generally unsatisfactory condition, the investment of private capital in individual residential structures within the inner loop is strongly discouraged. The development of new housing in the inner loop must occur in sufficiently large projects so as to create a new environment and offset the generally obsolete environment currently prevalent. Residential development on a neighborhood scale may best be created only through the medium of entrepreneurual [*sic*] action coupled with public action.[32]

This vision of large-scale residential development within the Inner Loop, built by a combination of public funding and private investment, took hold and was refined through the "paper blizzard" of planning activity that followed. Of the plans produced for downtown Rochester in the mid-1960s, the one that most effectively laid out a comprehensive blueprint for redevelopment was a federally funded plan called, aptly enough, "The Future of Downtown Rochester." This plan, also known as the General Neighborhood Renewal Plan (GNRP), was prepared by consultants based in Washington, DC, and Philadelphia and was completed in 1965. The consultants began with an inventory of downtown Rochester's strengths and weaknesses. On the plus side, they predicted growing employment and a stable retail base downtown, based on recent and planned developments that included the successful new Midtown Plaza and Midtown Tower; new bank buildings near Midtown and the Four Corners (west of the Genesee River); a planned new downtown headquarters for the Xerox Corporation; and projects underway for a new civic center, a federal office building, and a courthouse. They cast the nearly complete Inner Loop as a successful intervention that "will greatly improve access to and egress from" the central business district. Two urban renewal projects reshaping challenging areas of downtown were already underway (the Genesee Crossroads and Liberty Pole Green projects). The Eastman Theater remained a major cultural anchor in the heart of downtown.[33]

As for the downtown area's shortcomings: "As is typical of the central sections of American cities of comparable age, much of downtown Rochester is obsolete and deteriorated. Furthermore, the unplanned nature of its development during the nineteenth century has produced a disorganized pattern of buildings and streets."[34] Only about 40 percent of buildings within the central business district were considered to be in sound condition. Paradoxically, although 17 percent of land within the Inner Loop was used for surface parking, most of this was located at the periphery of the downtown area, creating the perception of a parking shortage at times of peak demand.[35]

To build on the downtown area's assets and address the deficits, the GNRP proposed a sweeping transformation of downtown to take place in the form of seven urban renewal projects in the next ten years. Together, the 7 projects encompassed 269 of the 418 acres within the Inner Loop. (Most of the other 149 acres were areas that had recently been redeveloped or were already undergoing renewal). For those 269 acres, the plan envisioned complete clearance and redevelopment for 102 and conservation activities for the other 167. Based on market studies, which, in turn, were based on an expectation of continued growth of the downtown office sector, the city's consultants predicted that demand for housing within the Inner Loop, as a whole, would grow by approximately 250 rental units per year from 1965 to 1975, for a total of about 2,550 units. They proposed a mix of 2,050 market-rate dwellings to be built by private developers, plus about 500 units to be built under special programs that subsidized housing construction for low-income and elderly residents. Housing was to be concentrated in two areas: in the southeast and northeast quadrants of the Inner Loop.

Based on the condition of existing buildings, the planners proposed two different approaches: retention of existing buildings plus new infill construction in

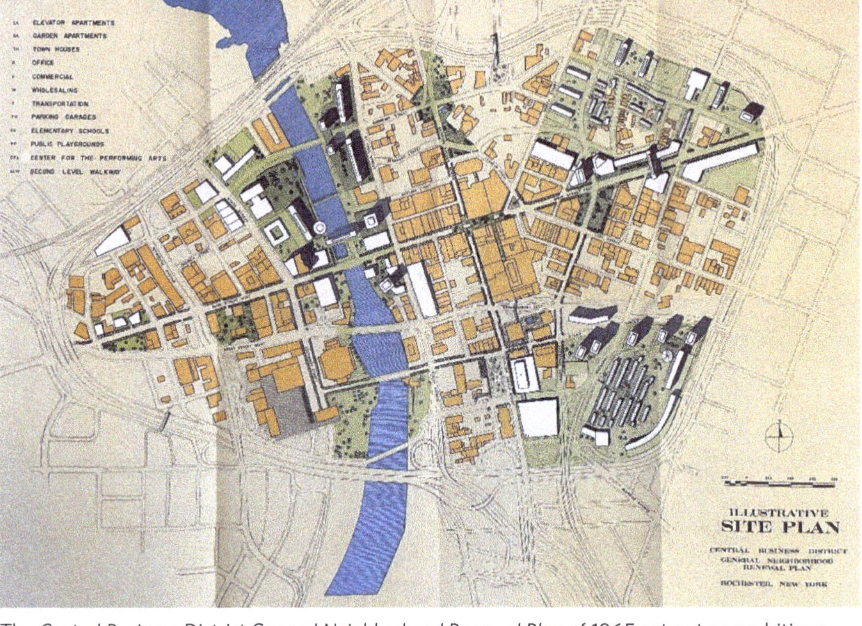

The *Central Business District General Neighborhood Renewal Plan* of 1965 set out an ambitious vision for transforming the area within the Inner Loop into a modern downtown defined by new buildings and an efficient transportation system. *The Future of Downtown Rochester: Central Business District General Neighborhood Renewal Plan, 1965 (City of Rochester, 1965).*

the Northeast Loop (better known today as the Grove Place neighborhood) and clearance followed by new construction in the Southeast Loop.[36] More than half of the housing the planners proposed for downtown Rochester was to be built in the Southeast Loop. This included 300 units in a proposed apartment-hotel, 1,100 in high-rise apartment buildings, and 150 in townhouses. In addition, the Southeast Loop redevelopment was to include a new school, a playground, an 800-space parking garage, 40,000 square feet of office space, and 75,000 square feet of commercial space. Other than the playground, the images included in the plan did not include any parks or public spaces.[37]

The GNRP offered a proposed timeline for the seven renewal projects, with the Southeast Loop identified as the first project the city should undertake. The planners offered several justifications for this prioritization.[38] On the positive side, planners believed that the imminent construction of the new Xerox headquarters at Broad and Chestnut Streets, across the street from the Southeast Loop, would increase the demand for downtown living. The planners did not, however, think that the existing housing stock of the Manhattan-Savannah area was worth saving. Housing-condition studies had shown that this neighborhood had the largest concentration of substandard housing in the city. Planners believed this "blight" was impeding city growth. Increasingly, newspaper articles pointed out the contrast between the sleek new office buildings being constructed for Xerox and other companies and the century-old housing just a block or two away. The GNRP included a full page of photographs that the authors considered illustrative of the deterioration and neglect in the neighborhood—conditions they described as "breeding grounds for a wide range of social problems."

Although Rochester had been known as a city where most people lived in one- and two-family houses, the *Central Business District General Neighborhood Renewal Plan* of 1965 put forth a vision of high-density downtown living, with sleek apartment towers and lively urban parks. *The Future of Downtown Rochester: Central Business District General Neighborhood Renewal Plan, 1965 (City of Rochester, 1965).*

While not explicitly stated at the time, the neighborhood's rapidly changing racial composition may also have been a factor in the priority given to the Southeast Loop, although the story here is more complicated than those in many other urban-renewal situations. In cities across the United States, the pejorative term "blight" was frequently used by white city leaders to describe neighborhoods with populations composed largely of immigrants, Puerto Ricans, and/or African Americans—regardless of the physical condition of the neighborhood—and used as a justification for aggressive urban-renewal action.[39] The author James Baldwin was among those who concluded that urban renewal was primarily a tactic to deliberately disperse predominantly Black neighborhoods: In a 1963 interview following a visit to San Francisco, he observed that "San Francisco is engaging, as . . . most northern cities are now engaged, in something called urban renewal, which means moving the Negroes out. It means Negro removal. That is what it means. And the federal government is an accomplice to this fact."[40] In Rochester, the inequities of urban renewal were similarly clear, at least to African American journalist Howard W. Coles, the editor and publisher

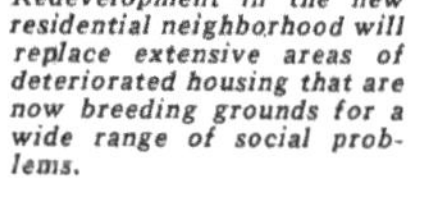

Redevelopment in the new residential neighborhood will replace extensive areas of deteriorated housing that are now breeding grounds for a wide range of social problems.

To make their case for demolishing almost every standing building in the Manhattan-Savannah neighborhood, planners publicized photographs that depicted conditions they claimed were pervasive in the area. *The Future of Downtown Rochester: Central Business District General Neighborhood Renewal Plan, 1965 (City of Rochester, 1965).*

of the *Rochester Voice* newspaper. A front-page article in his newspaper noted that areas like the Third Ward that were targeted for renewal were "some of the most valuable land within the city of Rochester. . . . This land or rather these land sites are going to sell sky high . . . to those that stand in with the politicians and the king makers. Many Negro and White home owners will never be able to buy another home again."[41]

Coles, who had long called for government intervention to provide better housing for African Americans, was critical of the way urban renewal was being conducted, advocated on behalf of families and businesses being displaced, and worked both within and outside of established systems to try to ameliorate disparities and injustices. He focused his attention on the Third and Seventh Wards, which historically housed the majority of Rochester's African American population, and while his general comments about the ulterior motives behind urban renewal can be applied to what was happening with the Southeast Loop project, he does not appear to have ever commented publicly on that project specifically.[42]

As noted above, the Manhattan-Savannah area was not a predominantly Black neighborhood, but it was rapidly changing from an almost all-white neighborhood to a racially mixed one, a situation planners, bankers, and real estate professionals generally viewed as a harbinger of decline.[43] While this was not a clear-cut case of "Negro removal," given that at least three-quarters of the residents were white, the suspicion that urban renewal projects were mostly intended to transfer valuable land in or near downtown from marginalized, low-income residents to well-connected developers was nevertheless apt. The cornerstone of the Southeast Loop plan, after all, was that a "blighted" area would be cleared of its buildings and residents so that private developers could construct mostly market-rate housing with the hope of enticing middle- and upper-middle-income people to live downtown.

The team of city staff and consultants that prepared the General Neighborhood Renewal Plan (GNRP) worked for another sixteen months to refine their vision for the Southeast Loop, unveiling their final plan for the ambitious $80 million project on September 1, 1966.[44] The plan was similar to what had been presented in the GNRP; the most notable change was that while the GNRP depicted a few blocks of buildings remaining standing along the north perimeter of the Southeast Loop, the 1966 plan called for the demolition of all but four buildings. Only the First Universalist Church on South Clinton Avenue, the University Club on Broadway, the Automobile Club on Chestnut Street, and the T. T. Bearing Co. building on Court Street were slated to remain standing.[45] The plan anticipated the relocation of 352 families and 115 businesses and the construction of 1,300 dwelling units, only 165 of which were to be "low-rent housing for adult families." The project was expected to get underway in 1968 and to be completed in the mid-1970s.[46]

By the time the city's plan was announced in September 1966, the Manhattan-Savannah neighborhood had already endured years of disruption. A few days after the formal unveiling, a reporter interviewed residents about their views on the project. Alice Leo, a twenty-six-year-old mother, said she had wanted to move out of the neighborhood since the Inner Loop construction made it unsafe for her children, but uncertainty about renewal made her house unmarketable: "The appraisers came around to look at the area . . . but they haven't given any prices, yet. Five years ago, we wanted to sell but we couldn't. Who wants to move in here? Now, we'll get a fair price from the city." Another mother, Frances Brown, said she was unhappy about renewal because she did not want to "live up too high," but she could not afford to live anywhere else that would allow children.[47] The neighborhood had many elderly residents who were averse to moving, such as eighty-year-old Russell Johnson, who had lived in the neighborhood for fourteen years and did not want to move to an apartment, saying, "They are not as nice as having a lawn." Albert Teal, another elderly resident, expressed a similar sentiment; he spent his time tending gardens in the neighborhood and said that even though the neighborhood was not what it used to be, many still had pride in it.[48] Gertrude Gerhard, a twenty-five-year resident of Savannah Street and the landlady of a neighboring house on Manhattan Street, summarized the neighbors' predicament: "I wouldn't put a dollar into this house. . . . Look at the trim. It needs painting. Twenty-five years ago this was a good neighborhood. Then, 10 years ago, they started to talk about the loop and they said they would be coming through here in a year. For 10 years now, we've been living here and wondering what they're going to do."[49]

Planners had not consulted with residents during the planning of the Southeast Loop project, and they gave very little consideration to the concerns of residents or property owners throughout the process. Faced with complaints from owners of well-kept commercial buildings on East Avenue that were proposed for demolition in the 1966 plan, despite having been seemingly spared in the 1965 GNRP, Richard Pine, the director of the Bureau of Redevelopment and Relocation in the Urban Renewal Department, responded that the city was justified in taking any building in the renewal area, whether it had been deemed substandard, in the interest of improving the city as a whole.[50] He was similarly unsympathetic to residents' fears, predicting that because the project would be spread out over several years and most residents of the area lived in two- or three-member households, finding new homes would not be difficult.[51]

Residents struggled to mount any defense to the planners. Although the city had failed to consult them throughout the planning process, once the plan was announced in September 1966, residents tried to get the attention of the city council and other decision-makers in the hope of getting more information and possibly having a say in the project going forward. City council member Robert Wood was sympathetic, noting his "distinct opinion" that residents "have not been sufficiently told what is going to happen to them, if anything."[52] As the project proceeded in fits and starts over the next several years, some residents organized protests in an attempt to draw attention to their concerns. While they won some limited concessions, such as better maintenance of a newly built playground at Manhattan and Broad Streets, they were unsuccessful in getting a meaningful voice in the planning process.[53] When the neighborhood was cleared, starting in 1968, residents scattered. Again referencing the block of houses that once stood where the Strong sits today, many of the white residents displaced by the project moved to other neighborhoods in the city, mostly in the northeast and southeast quadrants of the city. A few Black families moved to Corn Hill or the Nineteenth Ward, while others did not resurface in the Rochester City Directories. It is possible that some moved in with friends or family, while others may have left Rochester, perhaps returning to the South, the region in which many of the block's Black residents had been born.[54] Such a movement would have fallen in line with the post-1970 broader national trend of "reverse migration," which saw more than 100,000 African American southern migrants leaving locales in the North and West for southern states.[55]

The Failure of the Southeast Loop Plan

Even with a detailed plan, city planners failed to anticipate difficulties that arose throughout the project. The project started as planned, with the clearance of the southwestern portion of the neighborhood in 1968, but then construction largely stalled until 1970. The first reason for the delay was that the planners did not have a developer lined up. When clearance began in 1968, planners were optimistic that the city would be able to sell the land to private developers who would be eager to build market-rate housing in an "in-town" location. As it turned out, developers were never interested, having concluded that the type

This aerial photograph captured conditions when the Inner Loop was complete, clearance of the Manhattan-Savannah neighborhood was nearly complete, and redevelopment had not begun. *Rochester Bureau of Planning, Planning Study for In Town Area development, 1972 (City of Rochester, 1972).*

of housing the planners envisioned was not feasible. The cleared land remained vacant.[56] Then, in early 1971, the New York State Urban Development Corporation (UDC), a public authority created by the state legislature in 1968 with vast powers to undertake real estate development projects, became interested. It made an offer and showcased its own vision for the site in an exhibition at the Memorial Art Gallery.[57] The city took the offer.[58] In June 1971, the UDC started constructing the first building of the complex: a 198-unit apartment building for the elderly, situated on the corner of Broad and Manhattan Streets.[59]

Planners also ran into political struggles between the local, state, and federal governments, exacerbated by shifting federal priorities as the Nixon administration, which took office in 1969, adopted a different approach to urban issues than that of the previous Johnson administration. In 1970, Rochester enrolled its Southeast Loop project in the Model Cities Program in exchange for almost $3 million from the federal government.[60] Model Cities, developed under President Johnson, took a new approach to urban revitalization by funding both physical redevelopment programs and social and cultural programs, giving the local government more leeway to decide what activities to pursue.[61] While the program brought the project necessary funds, it also gave the federal Department of Housing and Urban Development (HUD) significant control over the project. Around the same time, Nixon's New Federalism, the policy of devolving considerable federal power to local municipalities, strengthened the City of Rochester's authority on matters of land use. Nixon believed the federal government should only do a post-audit review of local programs, decreasing the red tape that had been slowing Rochester's progress.[62]

While both the Model Cities Program and the New Federalism policies could have made it easier to push the project through the legal process, they inadvertently created significant conflict between the federal and local governments that ultimately slowed renewal. This played out in a difference of opinion over the sequencing of housing construction in the Southeast Loop. In 1968, the federal government approved the city's plan, which called for the construction of high-rent apartments as the first phase. In 1970, the city, then working with the UDC, submitted a revised plan prioritizing construction of lower- and moderate-income housing before luxury apartments. Optimism about Nixon's policies gave the city the confidence to move along with the modified plan before receiving federal approval. When the UDC began building two lower- to middle-income apartment buildings, HUD threatened to stop funding the project.[63] HUD objected to the revised plan because they had "serious reservations" over lower- and middle-income housing being built before upper-income housing—a move that city and UDC officials favored based on the city's desperate need for more affordable housing options. The regional HUD spokesman argued that if lower- and middle-income housing was built first, "there would be great difficulty in getting higher-income families to move into an area that was predominantly a lower-income development."[64] The UDC suggested a compromise: They would build some luxury units with the lower- and middle-income units and adjust based on results.[65] After six months of dispute, in September 1972 the city agreed to federal demands to first build luxury units and a six-acre park. HUD approved the plan.[66]

The city, the UDC, and HUD all believed a park was necessary for the success of the 700 luxury units.[67] The city agreed to fully fund the park, and—just

Manhattan Square Park (now Martin Luther King, Junior Park at Manhattan Square) was envisioned as a multi-level, modernist public space that would enhance a densely developed residential neighborhood. The park was built largely as designed, although the surrounding neighborhood did not fully materialize as planned. *Lawrence Halprin Associates, "South East Loop Park" (n.p., n.d. [1971]). City of Rochester.*

as leaders had done in 1888 when they hired Frederick Law Olmsted Sr. to design the city's first public parks—they selected one of the best landscape architects in the country to design not just a park, but a masterpiece of landscape architecture. The park plans, designed by preeminent landscape architect Lawrence Halprin, included an amphitheater, waterfalls, a fountain complex, a restaurant, an ice rink, and a monumental structure called the Space Frame.[68] In a report explaining the design, Halprin wrote:

> South East Loop Park has been designed with the understanding that the actual physical layout of a park is just the beginning—the activities and variety of experience that the people who use the park are able to create there is what completes it. . . . The goal was to include rather than restrict, to suggest rather than specify, and to leave ample room for spontaneous activity and change. . . . Potential user groups can be

> categorized as residents of the South East Loop Urban Renewal Area, downtown office workers, shoppers, occasional visitors, and tourists: there are also obvious age and time categories—anyone from infants to the elderly, and from those who will want five minutes in the open air to those who will want somewhere to spend all day.[69]

Halprin's bold, modernist design had its detractors, but ultimately the park, originally called Manhattan Square Park and now known as Dr. Martin Luther King Jr. Memorial Park at Manhattan Square, was built according to the design, opening in September 1975.

The broader project, meanwhile, hit rock bottom with the failures of its major developer and a key contractor. In January 1974, the local subcontractor who manufactured precast concrete panels for the apartment buildings filed for bankruptcy, forcing the construction of two buildings that were already underway to come to a halt. A few months later, the developer, Bennett, Pike, Brodsky Inc., backed out of its contract for three additional buildings that were in the planning stages. At this point, the UDC had only committed to 1,343 units.[70] In 1975, things got even worse. The UDC had financed its projects by issuing so-called moral obligation bonds, which, because the UDC was a state *authority* and not a state *agency*, meant that New York State did not have a legal obligation to pay bondholders back if the UDC couldn't do so. In reality, the state did have a "moral" obligation to do so, in that it couldn't in good conscience let the UDC default on those bonds. This business model, which assumed that the UDC would be able to repay bondholders once the projects started generating rent, enabled the UDC to take on ambitious projects that private developers considered too risky, but it ultimately caught up with the authority. In February 1975, the UDC ran out of money to complete the projects it had initiated, and state leaders had no choice but to use $200 million of taxpayer funds to repay bondholders.[71]

At this point, the city renewed its search for private developers, but given the struggling economy, there was no interest.[72] Less than a year later, the city took its final action on the project, demolishing eight buildings on East Avenue; the lots were to be left vacant for parking or grass.[73] In the end, only three of the eleven planned apartment buildings were constructed, all located just east of Manhattan Square Park: 10 Manhattan Square, a seventeen-story structure initially intended to be a "luxury" building but later lowered its rents when it did not attract enough middle-income residents; The Savannah, outfitted with low and moderate-income units; and Midtown Manor, an elderly residential community. All in all, instead of the planned 3,100 units, only 750 were developed.[74] A project that was meant to bring tax dollars back to the city instead cost more than $25 million in taxpayer money and displaced at least 125 families directly and many more indirectly.

In the early 1960s, planners had assumed there would be high demand for stylish new housing in a convenient downtown location within walking distance of new office buildings, parks, and shops. That expectation was probably a stretch even then, but it was definitely out of reach by the early 1970s, as perceptions of high crime, a distaste for high-density housing, and a preference for car-centric single-family housing dampened the demand for market-rate housing within the Inner Loop. The success of the Southeast Loop project was predicated on the city's ability to attract developers who believed they could make money on an ambitious, long-term housing project with a mix of high-end and low-income apartments. Private developers clearly signaled that they did not believe in this vision, and with no developer interest and no state or federal agencies able to take it on, the project was abandoned. And, as with so many urban renewal projects in Rochester and around the country, it was vulnerable city residents who suffered for other people's misjudgments and overreach.

A Lucky Rescue

In 1982, after writing the Southeast Loop project off as a failure, planners hit an unlikely jackpot. Margaret Woodbury Strong was born into a wealthy Rochester family in 1897. As a young girl, she traveled the world with her parents, collecting dolls and trinkets as she went. Throughout her life, she assembled a "Museum of Fascinations" in her Pittsford mansion, consisting of hundreds of thousands of objects she had collected during her travels. Upon her death in 1969, in accordance with her will, most of her $77 million estate was directed toward the creation of a museum to house her collection of dolls, toys, and other objects. In 1972, the trustees of the estate gave complete control of the entire collection to Director H. J. Swinney and tasked him with making Strong's wish a reality.

Swinney believed the mansion was too small to house the enormous collection, so he proposed an addition; however, in 1976, the trustees decided an addition was not feasible due to Pittsford's deed restrictions. In June 1977, the regents amended the charter to allow the trustees to build the museum anywhere in Monroe County. One month later, the trustees chose a parcel in

Southeast Loop Block III at 1 Manhattan Square as the building site. They liked the Southeast Loop for its vacant land and downtown location next to Manhattan Square Park. The location allowed for 200 parking spaces and plenty of room for the museum to expand in the future. The city, desperate for any builder, sold the 13.5 acres to the museum, embracing the museum leaders' enthusiasm for the project despite the fact that no marketing studies had been done to support the museum's predictions that up to 300,000 people a year would visit.[75]

The museum opened in 1982 and has been a huge success. After four expansions, it is now one of the largest history museums in the world and is arguably Rochester's top attraction.[76] While, in retrospect, the Strong National Museum of Play seems tailor-made for its downtown site, the museum was a serendipitous rescue for the failed urban renewal project. Without the pure luck of Strong's fortune, the project, like so many other urban renewal projects of its era, would be remembered only for its displacement, trauma, and failure. Today, with the east section of the Inner Loop filled and redeveloped, and with the mixed-use Neighborhood of Play taking shape around the museum (ironically helping to fulfill the ongoing need for quality housing that the failed urban renewal project had been intended to address), it is already hard to remember the years in which the museum sat almost alone amid a sea of parking and vacant land—let alone the neighborhood that was isolated and destabilized by the Inner Loop before being obliterated altogether.

Acknowledgments

This article began as a paper Benjamin Comeau wrote for a class he took during his sophomore year of college, "Transformations of Urban America." He received positive feedback (and an excellent grade) from his professor, who thought the Southeast Loop was an interesting and unusual urban renewal case study. Eggers Comeau, who had helped Comeau with his research by copying source materials in the Rochester Public Library's collection to send to him in Philadelphia, was also impressed and suggested they work together to turn the paper into an article. This is the first project this mother-son duo has worked on together. They would like to thank Emily Morry, PhD, for her excellent assistance and feedback throughout the process of turning a college paper into a *Rochester History* article. ■

1. Blake McKelvey, "Rochester in Retrospect and Prospect," *Rochester History* 23, no. 3 (July 1961): 25.
2. "State Maps Major Road Inside City," *Democrat and Chronicle*, March 25, 1946; and "Survey Eyes City Remade for Traffic," *Democrat and Chronicle*, July 7, 1946.
3. City Council Ordinance 48–410, in "City Planning Commission Scrapbook, 1944–1951," Local History & Genealogy Division, Rochester Public Library.
4. "City, State Decide to Start Arterial Highway Project," *Democrat and Chronicle*, October 23, 1948; and "These Dates Have Been Important in Rochester's Traffic Plan Job," *Democrat and Chronicle*, July 12, 1953.
5. The fifth section of the Inner Loop is the segment that was recently removed, filled, and redeveloped; as of this writing, plans are in the works to similarly eliminate the northern section. For a full explanation of the stages of Inner Loop construction, see Emily Morry's series of articles titled "Out of the Loop," parts 1 through 5, at the "Local History Rocs!" blog, rochistory.wordpress.com, published from August 2018 to March 2019.
6. Victor Gruen, *The Heart of Our Cities: The Urban Crisis: Diagnosis and Cure* (Simon and Schuster, 1964), 301–21; and Karen McCally, "The Life and Times of Midtown Plaza," *Rochester History* 69, no. 1 (Spring 2007).
7. Howard W. Coles published numerous articles about this topic in his publication, such as "Bad Housing Conditions! Prevail Here in Rochester," *The Voice*, February 28, 1938.
8. Blake McKelvey, "Housing and Urban Renewal: The Rochester Experience," *Rochester History* 27, no. 4 (October 1965), 11–13; and "Petitions Urge City to Obtain U.S. Housing Aid," *Democrat and Chronicle*, April 3, 1938.
9. These and other policies and tactics are described in Richard Rothstein, *The Color of Law: A Forgotten History of How Our Government Segregated America* (Liveright Publishing Corporation, 2017). Locally, Shane Weigand has done remarkable work documenting the use of racially restrictive covenants in neighborhoods in Rochester and Monroe County. A version of his presentation, shared many times in person and virtually, can be seen in PDF form at https://landmarksociety.org/wp-content/uploads/2019/05/ShaneWiegand_Redlining-Segregation_web.pdf or in video form at https://youtu.be/1fkL5vNkax8?si=AvCXEB9pXOiHEBnz and on other YouTube channels. See also *Confronting Racial Covenants; How They Segregated Monroe County and What to Do About Them: A Guide Provided by City Roots Community Land Trust and the Yale Environmental Protection Clinic* (City Roots Community Land Trust, 2020), available online at https://www.rochestersubway.com/topics/wp-content/uploads/Confronting-Racial-Covenants_Yale-City-Roots-Guide_2020-7-31.pdf.
10. Kurt Rohde and Pat Brasley, "Housing Discrimination Plagues Puerto Ricans," *Democrat and Chronicle*, January 15, 1955; and Eunice Grier and George Grier, *Negroes in Five New York Cities: A Study of Problems, Achievements, and Trends* (New York State Commission Against Discrimination, 1958), 80.
11. Citywide Survey, Phases 3B and 4, 47; and Brennon Thompson, "Race and Place in the Flower City," May 3, 2017, medium.com/@bt8002a/race-and-place-in-the-flower-city-300e8aac4d07.
12. "Harriman Approves Housing Authority Advised by Survey," *Democrat and Chronicle*, April 22, 1955.
13. *Report of the City of Rochester Rehabilitation Commission to the City Council*, December 1, 1957.
14. "Dwelling Inspectors Winding Up Survey in Sixth Ward Area," *Democrat and Chronicle*, March 1, 1957.
15. *Report of the City of Rochester Rehabilitation Commission to the City Council*, 1957, 1958, 1959.
16. *Rochester Rehabilitation Commission to City Council*; and "Self-Pride Essential in War on Slums," *Democrat and Chronicle*, October 19, 1957.
17. *Rochester Rehabilitation Commission to City Council.*

18. "Improvements Sought in Court Street Area," *Democrat and Chronicle*, April 8, 1956.
19. "Gettin' the Bloomin' Fourth in Bloom," *Democrat and Chronicle*, May 26, 1957.
20. "The Neighborhoods Nudge Us," *Democrat and Chronicle*, April 17, 1962.
21. "Fourth Ward Slams at Slums' Source," *Democrat and Chronicle*, January 27,1958; and "Rebuff on Blight," *Democrat and Chronicle*, March 3, 1958.
22. Cynthia Howk, former architectural research coordinator for the Landmark Society of Western New York, conversation with the authors, October 23, 2024.
23. US Census, City of Rochester, 1950, Enumeration District 69-27, accessed at ancestry.com.
24. Rochester City Directories, 1960, 1971. Historian Emily Morry has done painstaking research on the residents of the neighborhood; her research also found that there was rapid turnover of residents during this time period.
25. "Care, Not Jail, Urged for Chronic Alcoholics," *Democrat and Chronicle*, September 30, 1955.
26. Rohde and Brasley, "Housing Discrimination."
27. Karen McCally, "Building the Barrio: A Story of Rochester's Puerto Rican Pioneers," *Rochester History* 70, no. 2 (Fall 2007): 6–7.
28. Rohde and Brasley, "Housing Discrimination."
29. The authors located rental units costing $65 to $70 per month in several city neighborhoods, including Upper Falls, Maplewood, Swillburg, and Park Avenue.
30. "Survey Reports Rent-Gouging in Negro Welfare Housing," *Democrat and Chronicle*, November 13, 1961.
31. "Plans, Plans, Plans, Etc." *Democrat and Chronicle*, April 23, 1965.
32. Larry Smith and Co., *Rochester, N.Y. Market Analysis—Inner Loop Area*, prepared for City Planning Commission of Rochester, New York, 1960, 54.
33. Smith and Co., *Market Analysis*, 2–5.
34. Smith and Co., 7.
35. Smith and Co., 7–8.
36. Smith and Co., 37.
37. Smith and Co., 47–50.
38. The city of Rochester had already received a federal planning grant for a Southeast Loop project, so in that sense, the planners were justifying a fait accompli.
39. Andrew Herscher, "Black and Blight," in Irene Cheng et al., eds., *Race and Modern Architecture: A Critical History from the Enlightenment to the Present* (University of Pittsburgh Press, 2020), 291–307.
40. "A Conversation with James Baldwin," WGBH Educational Foundation, interview on May 24, 1963, broadcast on June 24, 1963, available online at the American Archive of Public Broadcasting, https://americanarchive.org/catalog/cpb-aacip_15-0v89g5gf5r.
41. "Urban Renewal Poised for Big, Big Steal," *The Rochester Voice* 32, no. 12.
42. The authors reviewed all available issues of Coles's publication from the years the Southeast Loop project was being planned and developed, as well as files in his archives at the Rochester Museum & Science Center pertaining to housing and urban development, and found no mention of the Southeast Loop, the Savannah-Manhattan neighborhood, or the Fourth Ward.
43. Rothstein, *The Color of Law*, 12.
44. Various articles used different project costs depending on whether they were including just the public funding (federal, state, and city) of about $22 million or also included the anticipated private investment, generally estimated at $50 to $60 million.
45. Peter Behr, "Southeast Renewal Unveiled," Rochester *Times-Union*, September 1, 1966. The Automobile Club building was ultimately demolished as part of the project; the other three remained standing, but only the church and the University Club, now the Inn on Broadway, survive today.
46. Department of Urban Renewal & Economic Development, *Progress Report, November 1967: Rochester's Urban Renewal Program* (City of Rochester, November 1967), 3–4.

47. "In the Shadow of Midtown," *Democrat and Chronicle*, September 8, 1966.
48. "Shadow of Midtown."
49. "Shadow of Midtown."
50. Behr, "Dozen Firms Fail in Bid to Escape Razing for Loop," Rochester *Times-Union*, October 17, 1966.
51. Mike Nauer, "Planners OK Loop Project, Ask Parking," *Democrat and Chronicle*, February 8, 1968.
52. "Meet on East Loop Area Renewal Plans Urged," *Democrat and Chronicle*, December 3, 1966.
53. "People Ask Renewal Voice," *Democrat and Chronicle*, March 26, 1968; "Protests May Stall Renewal," *Times-Union*, March 26, 1968; "Protests Win Loop Cleanup," Rochester *Times-Union*, July 25, 1968; Sue Smith, "Residents Barrage Officials at Southeast Loop Meeting," Rochester *Times-Union*, November 19, 1970; William D. Tammeus, "Center to Help Dislocated Persons," Rochester *Times-Union*, December 26, 1969.
54. Many thanks to Emily Morry of the Local History & Genealogy Division at the Rochester Public Library for conducting much of the research on neighborhood residents.
55. Research on block residents was conducted using Rochester City Directories and Ancestry.com; for more on reverse migration or the "New Great Migration," see Sabrina Pendergrass, "No Longer 'Bound for the Promised Land': African Americans' Religious Experiences in the Reversal of the Great Migration," *Race and Social Problems* 9, no. 1 (2017); William H. Frey, "The New Great Migration: Black Americans' Return to the South, 1965 to the present[sic]," *Brookings Institution*, brookings.edu; and Bruce J. Schulman, *The Seventies: The Great Shift in American Culture, Society, and Politics* (Grand Central Publishing, 2002).
56. William D. Tammeus, "Renewal Starts to Change Dying Area by Inner Loop," Rochester *Times-Union*, December 1, 1969.
57. "UDC Shows How It Gives Cities Another Chance," Rochester *Times-Union*, October 28, 1970.
58. "Loop Renewal Building May Begin in Late June," *Democrat and Chronicle*, May 28, 1971.
59. Gail Meadows, "Dirt Turned for Southeast Loop Project," *Democrat and Chronicle*, June 23, 1971.
60. "HUD Contract OK Due," Rochester *Times-Union*, July 14, 1970.
61. Victor A. Capoccia, "Chief Executive Review and Comment: A Preview of New Federalism in Rochester, New York," *Public Administration Review* 34, no. 5 (1974), accessed December 15, 2025, https://www.jstor.org/stable/975093.
62. Capoccia, "Chief Executive Review and Comment."
63. Steve Patranek, "City Loop Renewal Project Illegal," Rochester *Times-Union*, March 31, 1972.
64. Patranek, "City Loop Renewal Project Illegal."
65. Dan Lovely, "Let's Experiment with the Loop," *Democrat and Chronicle*, May 3, 1972.
66. Lovely, "Loop Project Is Approved," *Democrat and Chronicle*, September 27, 1972.
67. Tom Minnery, "City Hall Battle Brews of $3 Million Loop Park," Rochester *Times-Union*, April 17, 1973.
68. "Groups Fighting Loop Park Cuts," *Democrat and Chronicle*, June 12, 1973.
69. Lawrence Halprin Associates, "South East Loop Park," (n.p., n.d. [1971]).
70. "UDC Backs More Units," Rochester *Times-Union*, October 23, 1974.
71. A state commission that evaluated the UDC's failure and the resulting statewide fiscal crisis determined that while the UDC achieved notable successes, the organization's status as a public authority outside of the normal public and state oversight—and its leaders' assumptions and assertions that its projects would be financially self-sustaining, requiring no state funding—enabled it to overextend itself as it funded numerous risky projects with bonds that could not realistically be repaid without taxpayer money. See Moreland Act Commission on the Urban Development Corporation and Other State Financing Agencies, "Restoring Credit and Confidence: A Reform Program for New York State and its Public Authorities," March 31, 1976. Robert Caro's classic biography of Robert Moses, *The Power Broker*, provides context for

understanding the background of public authorities (also known as public benefit corporations), which were first used effectively in New York State in the 1920s to facilitate revenue-generating public works projects, but, primarily thanks to Moses, they were transformed into a largely unaccountable mechanism for pursuing transformative projects without regard for traditional public oversight.

72. John Machecek, "Downtown Decay Checked by Loop, Officials Say," Rochester *Times-Union*, May 2, 1976.
73. Stuart Elliot, "8 East Ave. Sites Coming Down," Rochester *Times-Union*, March 11, 1976.
74. Machecek, "Downtown Decay."
75. Michael Zeigler, "The Museum City?" *Democrat and Chronicle Upstate Magazine*, October 10, 1982, 8–10.
76. https://www.museumofplay.org/.

Richard Newman and Mark Ferrara Discuss the Erie Canal

Edited by Julia Resciniti

This is an edited transcription of an interview between RIT historian Richard Newman and Professor Mark Ferrara of SUNY Oneonta, whose book The Raging Erie: Life and Labor Along the Erie Canal *reexamines the many social and cultural impacts of the Erie Canal in the nineteenth century. The transcription retains the main features of the conversation.*

Richard Newman: *What is this book about? What are you hoping to get across, not only to specialists, people who study the Erie Canal, but general readers?*

Mark Ferrara: I focused the book on the years 1825 to about 1860 to 1861. So, basically the completion of the canal to the beginning of the Civil War. . . . I started to notice a tendency to romanticize the canal in the literature and to extol its virtues and to really celebrate the people who conceived it, the engineers who built it, the politicians who helped to push the legislation through, and people who grew wealthy along the canal corridor. But I noticed that there was a forgotten story there, which is the laboring poor and working classes who toiled almost invisibly along its corridors and suffered the slings and arrows, if you will, of a new emergent form of capitalism that was taking place along with the Industrial Revolution. And so I wanted to shine some light on the plight of the poor and working classes along the canal.

Newman: *So what was the big lesson that you learned after completing the book about the Erie Canal and New York State history more broadly?*

Ferrara: I mean, I think there's the kind of obvious answer to that, [which] is the economic transformation that happened in New York as a result of this small ditch that ran 363 miles from Albany to Buffalo, where boats travel just a few miles an hour. And yet it was the kind of information superhighway of its day and wrought all kinds of transformations. But I think in some ways, the big takeaways for me are a little bit darker. The child labor and exploitation of children, the animal abuse that happened along the canal, the prejudice against immigrants trying to assimilate into the country. And I think most shockingly of all for me . . . there was a constant struggle for Blacks to move out of any occupational positions that weren't unskilled and extremely low paying. And once we started to have a lot of German and Irish and other European immigrants coming in, a lot of the jobs that Black folk would do along the canal were taken over by the immigrants, so that [Blacks] were displaced occupationally after slavery was eradicated in the state.

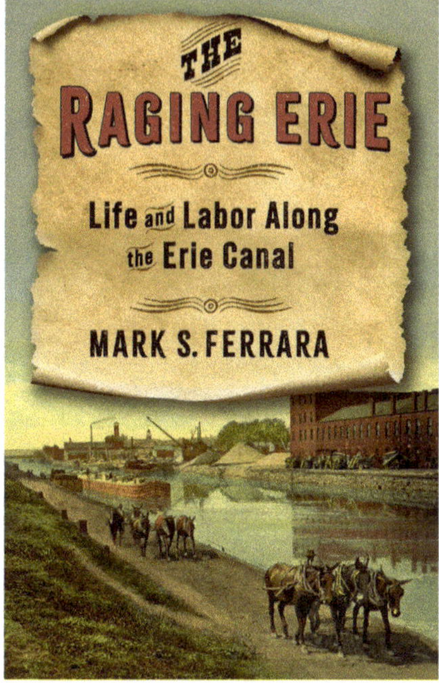

Newman: *Take us through some of the things you found on child labor, for example. You said that was one of the most disturbing things. Let's talk about some of the details. What did you find about life and labor relating to children along the Erie Canal?*

Ferrara: Yeah, the first thing is that there were a lot of children working along the Erie Canal, mostly boys, but sometimes girls dressed as boys. And they were often runaways, and they were often orphans. So they're the product of dysfunctional families. We're talking about, as you know, a time period in American history where there was a lot of drinking going on, and that contributed to domestic violence. And we're also talking about a time when every family member has to contribute to the income of a family to keep it afloat. So that included children selling newspapers, blackening boots, scrounging and scavenging for junk metal. And so, if a father died or was injured on the job, a huge portion of family income would be lost. Same for the mother, and same for the kids, in some sense. And there were no social safety nets. [So] what does a child do when a father's abusive, or [when] one or both parents dies? A lot of the children along the canal were not orphaned completely. They lost one parent, but it was enough to disrupt their lives to the point that they were willing to leave home and work on the canal for $10 a month, usually doing, I mean, they're most associated with the towpaths and leading the mules and horses that pulled the boats along the canal. And they worked six hours on, six hours off, called a trick, six to seven days a week. And in the winter, there's no work, so they could have been stranded somewhere along the canal corridor. There are stories of unscrupulous boat captains not paying the children at the end of the season. There are stories of children dying after being pulled from the towpath into the canal, and other injuries, but also from exposure in the winter. There are even stories of children ending up in prisons or jails during the winter season just to get by. So when we think about the Erie Canal, we don't usually think about that level of suffering. Now, for boat children, captains of the boat, life was a little easier. Still, I mean, there's no constant school that you can go to. Medical care is difficult. Children did fall in and drown in the canal. In fact, you can see pictures from the second half of the nineteenth century of children with ropes on the boat, with ropes tied around them, so in case they did fall in, they could be retrieved pretty easily. But the labor of children pulling boats along the canal was an integral part of the prosperity of the canal, but it's one of those facets that kind of gets lost. We forget that children served

Child leading mules on C & O Canal Towpath. In the nineteenth and early twentieth centuries, animal and child labor were essential to the operation of the Eric Canal, like other canals. *Chesapeake and Ohio Canal National Historical Park, NPS Collection, no date.*

whiskey to workers who were partly paid in whiskey, and they also did more dangerous jobs, like setting off explosives, and a lot of orphan children lost their lives, but they also didn't have people coming to ask after them after they were injured or killed. There is not equal shared prosperity going on, and maybe there are resonances to income inequality today as well. Obviously, those were different times. We're a different nation, but we are going through a period of income inequality that we have to reach back to the Gilded Age to find a parallel. Yes, so farmers along the canal were very lucky. People who could own boats, people who were lock tenders would do pretty well. There are a lot of businesses and people that prospered, people who invested in the canal, people who bought the bonds. So there's a lot of wealth being generated, but it's not being generated for children, immigrants, workers along the canal. They're really being exploited by this early form of American capitalism. It's an industrial revolution, but it's also displacing families. You're moving from the farm and family as an economic unit to wage labor or wage slavery, if you like, where jobs didn't pay a breadwinner enough to support a family. During economic crises, wages went down. Competition from immigrants was particularly tough along the canal corridor. So for all the prosperity generated, which was enormous, it didn't trickle down to the folks that we're talking about, the poor and working classes who labored pretty anonymously along the canal corridor.

Young boy tethered to the deck of a canal boat to prevent him from falling overboard, Chesapeake and Ohio Canal, circa 1910–1924. The C&O Canal runs along the Potomac River from Washington, DC, to Cumberland, Maryland. Accounts of the Erie Canal also describe small children being tied to the boats for safety. *Photograph by E. B. Thompson, NPS History Collection, HFCA 1174.*

Newman: *It really does seem to be a preview of things to come in Silicon Valley or the financial sector of New York City. Tons of wealth, but not evenly distributed. And in many ways, that's the point. Not everyone gains from this galloping hyper-capitalism.*
Ferrara: Yeah, precisely.

Newman: *Let's talk about a few of the other communities that you examine here, particularly a group that often gets left out in histories that deal with economics in the mid-nineteenth century, Native Americans.*
Ferrara: I start the book with a discussion of the Haudenosaunee. And I go back a couple hundred years before the canal's built to try to look at those communities and what they were like, and to make the important point that New York State was Native American. And little by little, they were displaced. DeWitt Clinton's journal makes some passing references to Native Americans, whom he calls Indians . . . but this is 1810. And I think he's—if memory serves—somewhere in the Rome area. And he's making this comment that here's this territory that used to belong to these proud Native American peoples, and there's hardly any of them to be seen as he's traveling westward through the interior of the state, which is still very wild, alright? And that really struck me. I had done the research on the book chapter, so I knew it. But 1810, you know, you're already talking about the kind of forced displacement of [Native] peoples. And a lot of it, as my chapter goes through. There's a lot of trickery and fraud perpetrated against them to take lands at very low prices. And that continues right up until the canal is completed, even a little bit after, like into the 1830s. So that by then, you have a large-scale displacement of Native peoples and their confinement to small reservations around the state that may still be familiar to some of the people listening to this exchange. So it is sad—it is another sad part of the Erie Canal story. And of course, they're losing their way of life as Europeans start fencing off, you know, taking more and more land. Traditional ways of hunting and living are displaced. And so, yeah, I felt it was very important to start with the Haudenosaunee before we even got into telling the story of the canal at all.

Newman: *Let's talk a little bit about women and the Erie Canal, which is yet another significant theme. What did you find there?*
Ferrara: It's hard to even know where to start, but legally, the status of women was tied to English common law [and

its principle of coverture], and so there's a series of emancipation efforts and legislation that's slowly giving women rights throughout the first half of the nineteenth century. But early in the century, we're really operating under a paradigm where the husband and wife are one [legal] entity, basically the husband, where we have women who might not be able to inherit property, may not be able to enter into legal agreements on their own, who are, when they do work, either inside the home, doing piecework kind of stuff, or outside of the home, they're being paid wages that are lower than men, of course. And they're doing all kinds of free labor at home, too, that's essential. Sometimes they're taking in boarders. Sometimes they're doing work inside the house. They're taking care of children, too. On the Erie Canal, you can find them cooking on boats, for example, cooking for camps, doing laundry. [And] prostitution is another subject that kind of comes up when we start talking about the experience of women during this time period and along the canal corridor. I think the last chapter in my book is on vice along the canal. And so there's a pretty long treatment of the socioeconomic factors that drove women and young girls into prostitution during this time. And some of the voices that I capture are young women—thirteen, fourteen, fifteen years old, sometimes orphaned, who are using prostitution as a way to get by. So, yeah, it's a complex story. A lot of these chapters can be kind of opened up. This summer, I've been working on a paper taking another look at Black labor along the Erie Canal. . . . I was in Lyons last year and had a question from a gentleman. He was asking me how many slaves dug the canal. And I was like, "I don't know, I'm really not sure." And we're not sure because of the way records were kept and a lot of other factors. It's difficult to answer definitively some of these questions. So, I was able to find a couple newspaper reports that suggested Black laborers, in the early days of canal construction, so 1817 to 1819–1820, did work alongside white laborers. There are reports of racial strife all the way back then. But it's not clear how many were slaves and how many were free Blacks. So that gets murky. Census documents are problematic to the researcher because Blacks are living a very itinerant existence along the canal corridor. They're living in marginalized places where census takers might not go. And they're sometimes actively avoiding white census takers. So, it's even difficult in the early part of canal history to get an idea of how many Blacks were living in Rochester in 1820, 1825. You can look at the records, and there are records, but then you have to ask yourself, "Well, this is probably being undercounted." And then that situation gets compounded when you try to look at Black life in smaller towns along the canal, like Geneva, for example, or Lyons. And then recordkeeping gets even more difficult. And so maybe, in general, what one has to do for a project like this is to look at other ways of getting at this kind of information—beyond census records and newspaper reports. And newspaper reports can be helpful, but they can also be problematic, for a variety of reasons, and unreliable. And after the Civil War, you get salacious press and exaggerated reports of all kinds of things, so the historian has to be very careful about taking things at face value. As I was saying earlier, I was just shocked by the marginalization, by the racism, that was just perpetual. And during the period I was writing about, so 1825 to 1860, roughly—it's like there's no break. It's like, oh, good, slavery's over. In 1827, we can finally join society as equal members.

No, you can't. And you're going to be relegated to certain kinds of professions, and they are going to be lower-paying professions. And there's going to be very few, 2 percent-ish of, Blacks who were able to own property enough to vote, so they're disenfranchised that way, too. So, I kept kind of putting myself in that position, if it makes sense, and just thinking about the constant marginalization, the constant disenfranchisement, the lack of opportunity that Black Americans experienced along the canal corridor. And this is without even getting into the Fugitive Slave Act of 1850. Slaves escaping from the South and expecting to find something much better—only to discover some of the difficulties they faced in the Plantation South had [their] own kind of correlates up North. So, it's a distressing topic, but it seems like one that it's important to kind of go back in there and to have another look at what life looked like and to reconsider the North as this haven, or New York State particularly, as a haven for free Blacks, Blacks that are escaping slavery, and to reconsider that story a little bit. It's kind of looking at the other side of American prosperity, where we can celebrate [that prosperity], and it deserves to be celebrated in many ways. The Erie Canal is an amazing thing. You can bike, hike, kayak; it's amazing. And when we think about the economic transformations abroad, it is amazing, but we often don't think about it as a site of trauma and sorrow as much as triumph. And I think that's hopefully the contribution of the book is to offer a different take while still acknowledging all of the positives that came out of the canal and canal life.

Newman: *So let's end with this. If you had one recommendation for people in Rochester about how they should think about commemorating the canal through the aqueduct or ruins, because there's a lot of conversation about this now, what should they be thinking?*

Ferrara: We want to celebrate these achievements, and we want to recognize that the Erie Canal created Rochester as one of the original boomtowns. But I hope there'll be room in those celebrations for some acknowledgment of the types of issues that we've been talking about during our conversation. If we could remember some of the children who worked along the towpath, and not romanticize their plight, but to remember it as a kind of sacrifice upon which our current prosperity is partially built. Ditto for women, ditto for African Americans along the canal corridor. And I think there's even a place in our heart for the abuse that animals would have endured along the canal, horses in particular. I think there's room to remember Native American displacement and other forms of social trauma. The immigrants who came and toiled literally on the margins of society in shanty towns, in the city, in places like Five Points, in slum areas, [packed] sixteen into a room. All of these are experiences that contributed to the success of the canal. And there are a lot of people who gave their labor and life to working and building along the canal. We sometimes are apt to forget that, especially when we're celebrating a bicentennial and something as monumental as the completion of the Erie Canal.

Newman: *I think that's a powerful statement. Once again, Mark Ferrara, thanks for joining us for this talk. The book is wonderful. For people who are reading this or listening to it, once again, it's called* The Raging Erie: Life and Labor Along the Erie Canal. ■

BOOK REVIEW

The Roots of Flower City: Horticulture, Empire and the Remaking of Rochester, New York

by Camden Burd. Ithaca: Cornell University Press, 2024.

Matt Dallos

Horticulture held significant economic and cultural value in nineteenth-century America. Scientists, home gardeners, and even politicians argued that horticulture would civilize and beautify the young nation. Camden Burd's *The Roots of Flower City: Horticulture, Empire, and the Remaking of Rochester, New York*, published in 2024, focuses on the supply side of horticulture by investigating the shifting fortunes, cultural power, and nationwide ecological effects of plant nurseries in Rochester during the nineteenth and early twentieth centuries. The result is a well-written, engaging book that situates Rochester as a key city within a national history of plant selling. Burd links commercial plant distribution to settler colonialism in the history of the American West; he also integrates economics and ecology to allow for the presence of other-than-human historical actors such as an insect pest known as San Jose scale.

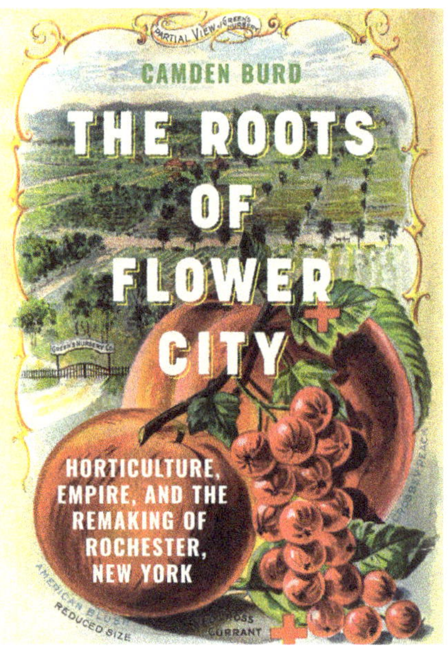

Burd, an assistant professor at Clemson University, argues that nursery owners in Rochester were significant agents of environmental change in nineteenth- and early twentieth-century America. By supplying plants to settlers, the nursery owners were able to facilitate the planting of a European-influenced notion of landscape improvement across the nation. They not only sold plants; they shifted ecologies. Burd makes this compelling argument by tracing the rise of Rochester-based nursery owners' economic success and cultural importance

Matt Dallos, PhD, is an assistant professor of Landscape Architecture at SUNY College of Environmental Science and Forestry in Syracuse, New York, and the owner of Thicket Workshop, a plant-focused design firm in Ithaca, New York.

during the middle and late decades of the nineteenth century. By leveraging sales agents, transportation networks, and cultural cachet, these nursery owners made significant profits by shipping large volumes of plants across the nation. Their business footprints expanded significantly to accommodate this growth, and soon a few—primary among them Mount Hope Nursery, owned by George Ellwanger and Patrick Barry—had amassed real estate empires within Rochester. The resulting wealth permitted these business owners to gain significant influence within the city, turning a few neighborhoods, including what is today known as Highland Park, into examples of how a more horticulturally minded, foliage-filled city might benefit its citizens in an era of social reform. These smaller-scale horticultural efforts would eventually boost support for the development of Rochester's park system, designed by Frederick Law Olmsted. The city ultimately gained a reputation as a sort of model horticultural city. But after the turn of the twentieth century, following the accidental dispersal—from orchards in various parts of the country—in shipped nursery stock of an invasive pest, the San Jose scale, that damaged orchards, the long-distance shipping of plants was crimped by negative press and quarantine legislation. This contributed to a decline in nursery profits that was compounded by an economic downturn. The nursery business in Rochester faltered, and the owners lost their influence.

Burd uses the label "ecological empire" to describe the ideals, actions, and material effects of the research, sales, and distribution efforts made by nursery owners. According to Burd, these individuals were shaping the environments of lands recently (and often violently) settled by Europeans. It's a compelling point to make, as it reframes the shipping of, say, 100 Northern Spy apple trees or 50 Boxwood shrubs from rote-order fulfillment to active ecological conquest—part of the broader nationalistic project to remake the environments of the growing nation to match cultural and market-based expectations. But "ecological empire" in the context of this book would have benefited from further development. How, for example, was the imported, Eurocentric vision of a horticultural Eden applied to the often-harsh climates of the American West, where many plants were shipped? When plants—which have limitations in the climate and soils in which they can grow—were shipped into harsh environments, what points of friction arose between ideals and reality? What did the resulting hybrid landscapes look like? How did settlers view them? Without these further levels of detail, "ecological empire" is at risk of being viewed as a seamless, uncontested process. Additional granularity in "ecological empire," as applied to the particular story of this book, would have helped further establish the book's arguments.

Although this book is centered around Rochester and its environmental, economic, and social particularities, Burd successfully places this study within a broader national context. A reader understands the specific manifestations of this history in Rochester while also understanding the wider causes and effects. This approach is also visible in the way that Burd approaches certain sources. Nursery sales logs might initially seem to be a rather provincial set of documents. But when Burd contextualizes these documents within nationwide economic, cultural, and ecological events, they offer nuanced insight into those broader historical moments. Because of this combination of local and national contexts, the book should interest readers who already hold an understanding and appreciation of Rochester's history, since it would be helpful in considering the city's history through both a narrower horticultural lens and a wider national lens. Of particular note are in-text maps that chart the geographic distribution of nursery sales, displaying the reach of Rochester's nurseries. The book will also be of interest to environmental historians, historians of the nineteenth and early twentieth centuries, and historians of capitalism—perhaps even architectural and landscape historians, given a recent shift toward questions of plant life and labor within those areas.

The Roots of Flower City also furthers an important scholarly shift. Environmental historians have often given minimal attention to horticulture. In the 1980s and 1990s, the field was more focused on topics related to the environmental movement, such as wilderness areas and environmental policy. Even in the 2000s' and early 2010s' turn toward complex hybrid environments that blend natural processes and anthropogenic processes, horticulture continued to be slighted. *The Roots of Flower City* places horticulture centrally within the field, contributing to an existing literature that argues for horticulture to occupy a more significant place within the historical scholarship of American culture and the natural world, including through books such as Philip J. Pauly's 2007 *Fruits and Plains: The Horticultural Transformation of America* and Shen Hou's 2013 *The City Natural: Garden and Forest Magazine and the Rise of American Environmentalism*. Further, *The Roots of Flower City* brings together capitalism, economics, culture, environment, and locality in a way that offers a methodology for future horticultural-focused studies to build upon. ■

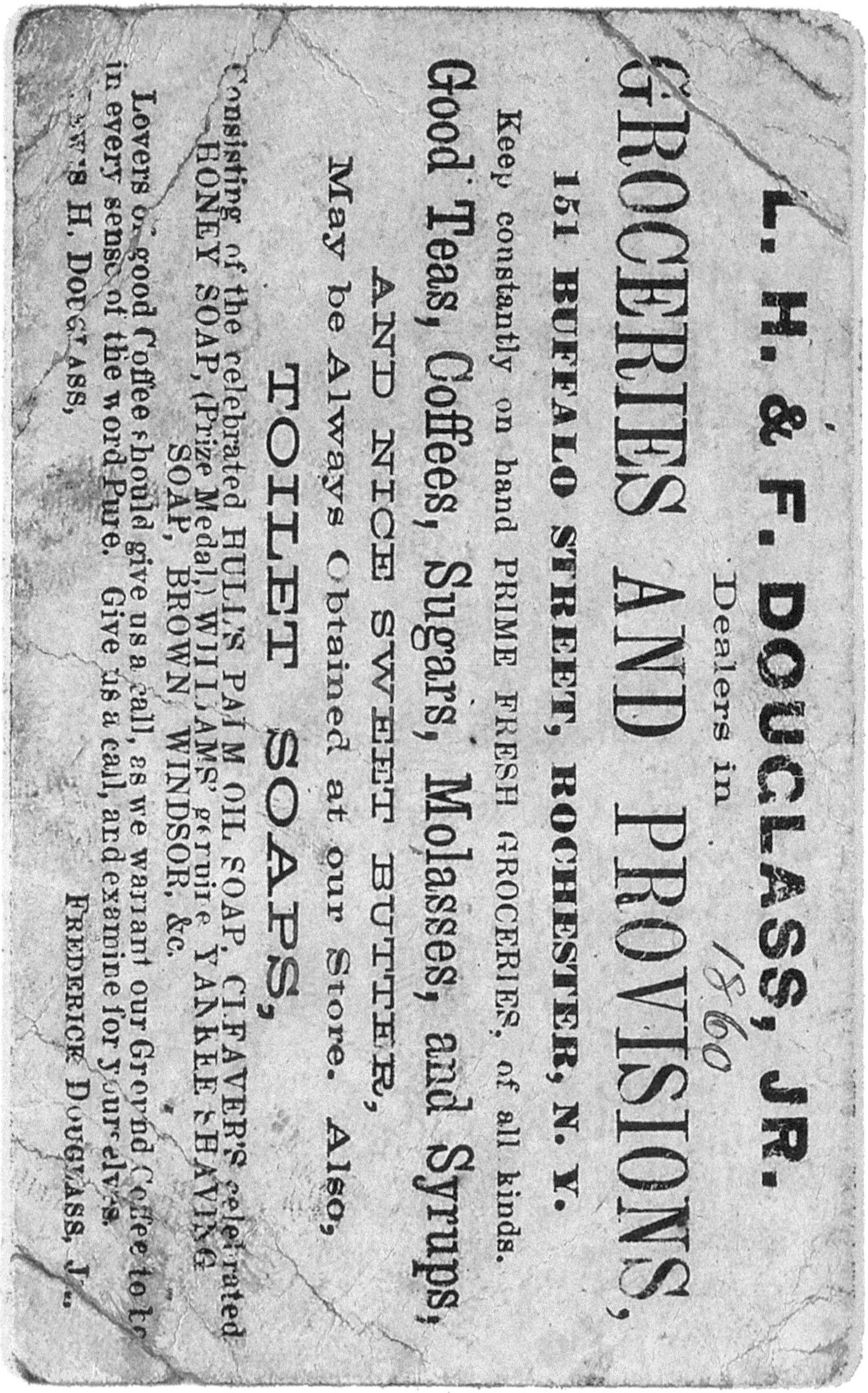

L. H. & F. DOUGLASS, JR.

Dealers in 1860

GROCERIES AND PROVISIONS,

151 BUFFALO STREET, ROCHESTER, N. Y.

Keep constantly on hand PRIME FRESH GROCERIES, of all kinds.

Good Teas, Coffees, Sugars, Molasses, and Syrups,

AND NICE SWEET BUTTER,

May be Always Obtained at our Store. Also,

TOILET SOAPS,

Consisting of the celebrated HULL'S PALM OIL SOAP, CLEAVER'S celebrated HONEY SOAP, (Prize Medal,) WILLIAMS' genuine YANKEE SHAVING SOAP, BROWN WINDSOR, &c.

Lovers of good Coffee should give us a call, as we warrant our Ground Coffee to be in every sense of the word Pure. Give us a call, and examine for yourselves.

LEWIS H. DOUGLASS, FREDERICK DOUGLASS, JR.

Douglass Brothers' Grocery

Harold J. Schuler

Philanthropist and former surgeon Walter O. Evans began collecting African American art, literature, and other artifacts in the 1970s. The daunting collection he amassed over the course of his lifetime includes more than 100,000 books and manuscripts, as well as a substantial number of items connected to Frederick Douglass and his family.

Letters from the collection appear in the 2018 book *If I Survive: Frederick Douglass and Family in the Walter O. Evans Collection* by Celeste-Marie Bernier and Andrew Taylor. The work represented the first time much of this material had become generally available to the public. One item in particular shed light on a little-known aspect of the Douglass family's history.

Included in the book is a circa 1890 letter in which Frederick Douglass Jr. recalled: "At the age of 18, I went into the Grocery business in Rochester, on the corner of Buffalo and Sophia Streets."[1] (Today, the location would be West Main Street and Plymouth Avenue.)

The 1861 Rochester City Directory lists the store in question, but prior to this letter's publication, little else was known about the store, which also involved Frederick Jr.'s brother Lewis H. Douglass.

The Walter O. Evans Collection of Frederick Douglass and Douglass Family Papers, acquired by Yale's Beinecke Rare Books and Manuscript Library in February 2020, provided another piece to this historical puzzle. Contained in one of the collection's scrapbooks is a business card for "L. H. & F. Douglass Jr. Dealers in Groceries and Provisions, 151 Buffalo Street, Rochester N. Y."

The card confirmed the business's existence, and a follow-up search through the advertisement sections of two nineteenth-century newspapers, the Rochester *Union and Advertiser* and *Rochester Daily Democrat*, revealed ads for the Douglass store in several issues between September 1860 and July 1861.

So why did the Douglass brothers enter the grocery business in 1860, and why was the venture so short-lived? The answer to the first question may lie in part with local demographic trends. Rochester's African American population began growing steadily following the opening of the Erie Canal in 1825. Between 1840 and 1850, the city witnessed a jump from 450 to 549 Black residents. The following decade, however, 1 in 4 Black residents *left* the city, with just 410 African Americans

Opposite: Circa 1860 business card for the Douglass brothers' grocery store. *Walter O. Evans Collection of Frederick Douglass and Douglass Family Papers. James Weldon Johnson Collection in the Yale Collection of American Literature, Beinecke Rare Book and Manuscript Library.*

calling Rochester home by 1860, the year the Douglass brothers launched their business.[2]

As the Black population declined, so, too, did the number of Black grocers. Although there were four Black grocers in the city in 1850, none remained by 1860. Lewis and Frederick Douglass Jr.'s store, then, certainly filled a void in the local African American community.

The reason Rochester had lost a substantial number of African American residents, grocers included, in the 1850s was largely owing to a combination of two factors: First, the decade witnessed a massive influx of Irish immigrants. Between 1850 and 1855, Rochester's Irish population doubled; by 1860, the Irish-born and their children represented about a fourth of the city's entire population. These recent immigrants competed with local African Americans for jobs, drastically reducing their numbers in several fields of employment. With fewer opportunities in both skilled and unskilled positions, many Black people in Rochester chose to relocate elsewhere in the 1850s.[3]

Perhaps more important was the passage of the Fugitive Slave Act in 1850, which required that all escaped enslaved people be returned to their enslavers. Moreover, any citizen assisting a runaway enslaved person faced a penalty of six months' imprisonment and a $1,000 fine.

The Fugitive Slave Act called into question the security of even free African Americans living in Northern communities such as Rochester. As Douglass's biographer Benjamin Quarles noted, "Douglass was legally free, but to him and many others with pigmented skins the first six months after 'the whirlwind and the pestilence set in' were six of the gloomiest months of their existence." Quarles postulated that during this time period, "perhaps a total of nine thousand—who had been living in fancied security[,] hastened across the border to Canada."[4]

While the Douglass family remained in Rochester, they moved from their Alexander Street residence to a new home on the outskirts of the city at the end of 1851, perhaps so that they could continue to harbor freedom seekers in a more hidden and secretive manner.[5]

The South Avenue house was just under two miles from the Douglass Brothers' grocery store at 151 Buffalo Street. The grocery store, in turn, was a few blocks from the Talman Building, where Frederick Douglass published his three newspapers, *The North Star*, *Frederick Douglass' Paper*, and *Douglass' Monthly*. Frederick Douglass Jr. would make the move down the street and begin helping his father run the latter paper in 1861.[6]

Whether the career change prompted the grocery store's closure that same year or vice versa is not known, but both Frederick Jr. and Lewis would soon turn their attention to the Civil War, with Frederick Jr. helping raise the Massachusetts 54th and 55th infantry regiments and the 5th Massachusetts Cavalry, while Lewis became a sergeant major in the 54th regiment.

It seems that Frederick Douglass Jr.'s interest in the grocery trade carried through the postwar years. As his obituary notes, after spending a few years in Denver, "he came to Washington [DC] and opened a small grocery store that stood for years in the grounds now occupied by the house in which he died."[7] ■

1. Celeste-Marie Bernier and Andrew Taylor, *If I Survive: Frederick Douglass and Family in the Walter O. Evans Collection* (Edinburgh, UK: University of Edinburgh Press, 2018), 633.
2. Monique Patenaude, *Bound by Pride and Prejudice: Black Life in Frederick Douglass's New York* (University of Rochester, PhD Dissertation, 2013).
3. Blake McKelvey, "The Irish in Rochester: An Historical Retrospect," *Rochester History* 29, no. 4: 6; Patenaude, *Bound by Pride and Prejudice.*
4. Benjamin Quarles, *Frederick Douglass* (Washington, DC: Associated Publishers, 1948), 114–15.
5. While still living at the Alexander Street house in September 1851, the Douglass family provided shelter to three high-profile freedom seekers who had been involved in an armed resistance in Christiana, Pennsylvania. The event would become known as the "Christiana Resistance." See Frederick Douglass, *Life and Times of Frederick Douglass* (Hartford, CT: Park Publishing Co, 1881), 349–50. The turmoil caused by this incident may have provided the impetus for Douglass to move his family to the South Avenue property within three months. Douglass would later purchase the property in March 1854.
6. Bernier and Taylor, *If I Survive*, 633.
7. The Washington *Evening Star,* July 28, 1892.

www.ingramcontent.com/pod-product-compliance
Lightning Source LLC
LaVergne TN
LVHW052349100826
845147LV00012B/795
* 9 7 8 1 9 5 6 3 1 3 4 9 9 *